I0439864

Being a Woman

by

Pamela Ann Smith

**Your self-worth and how you see yourself
is the key to all your rights; if you do not
feel that you are worthy, then you will not
be seen as worth the right.**

Pamela Ann Smith

ISBN: 10-1481149059

ISBN: 13-978-1481149051

To all those women who came before us and fought with all their might to enable us to have the rights we have today.

To all the celebrated woman of today who continue to fight for a woman's worth, so that we may feel worthy of the empowerment for tomorrow.

To all the women of tomorrow who will continue to move forward, keeping and protecting our sacred rights.

Contents

Preface

I was born in England, which was my home until I was twenty-one years old; I was always a bit of a free spirit, and so at seventeen years old I enlisted in the WRAF (Women's Royal Air force) for four years. Near the end of my term I married, and then came to the US in 1966. This was the age of the sexual revolution, and much of the world at that time was in full blast over the Vietnam War, civil rights, and women's rights issues.

I have always had a desire to write, and I eventually wrote a family history book for my children as a legacy for them. I have completed photographic specialty books and still wanted to do more.

Life kept me very busy, being a wife and mother, going to college for my RN degree, and all my many other duties.

The years seemed to have flown by, and now I find myself with some time to let my passion for writing flow. The subject of women's rights, its beginnings, and how far we have come over the generations suddenly opened itself to me during the course of the last presidential campaign.

As a seasoned woman in my sixties, I have never been more aware of the viability of woman's rights as I am today. I am an ordinary middle-class woman; I have been a registered nurse for three decades, working in many arenas of health care. I have also had my own skin-care practice. I love to share my knowledge with others, and, if it helped, then I was happy. I continue to be the bearer of a California esthetician's license. I have written many (unpublished) articles on the subject of skin care and have given several presentations to small groups and clients on the subject. I have been a working mom and grandmother, just like the rest of you, and I am just being the best that I can be. I have been so busy with life, like everyone else, raising my three children and welcoming six grandchildren into the world. So now, after all that time, as they say, "it is never too late." Or, should I say, "all good things come to those that wait"? I now will pursue my passion and dream of writing.

My Goal: What exactly am I trying to achieve with the contents of this book? Well, for starters, I have come to see that many women in certain age groups today do not really think about what rights they have; they just have them. They may have heard a snippet here and there of something their ancestors fought for, but still, the information is all fragmented. They have been born with these rights—that is what women have always fought for—so are we talking about an amazing success? *Yes*, we are, and so this book is in *honor* of all the women who gained those rights for us over the years gone by. I feel that vital history is getting lost in time somehow, and it wasn't that long ago!

I wanted to compile my research and studies in one easy-to-read book, so that when you reach the end, you will be inspired and wealthy with the knowledge of what *being a women* in today's world means, so you can understand how we got to where we are today and be aware of the unleashed strengths you may have.

All this, so you can feel the pride and self-worth that the women before you felt while they struggled to get us the rights we have today.

My years of developed wisdom have come to show me that the core of who you are is in knowing yourself and being true to your values and principles. All that in turn will show you who you are and what your direction in life will be. The pioneer women before us, *they had that*, and that is why they were able to give us our gifts of equality and freedom that we have today. They showed us the way and want us to continue their work, so, if you can believe in yourself, as they did, you will know that

all things are possible.

CHAPTER 1

Being a Woman

Yes, women's rights have come a long way, but is it realized just how far and what a struggle the journey has been?

Not so long ago, I asked a lovely young woman in her forties why she was so upset with the words *women's liberation movements*; she answered, "They are trying to change the way men treat us."

"In what way?" I asked.

"Well," she answered, "one example would be that the man would not treat me like a lady anymore and wouldn't want to pay for my meal when taking me out."

In astonishment, I replied, "*No*, this is about women's rights, not courtesy!"

She answered, "What *rights*! I *have* rights; what more are there?"

I took a deep breath and said, *"Read my book!"*

This book is an overview of feminist history, reflecting the equal rights' struggles that women have endured through the days of suffrage in the nineteen hundreds for the vote, thus winning the Nineteenth Amendment for us all in 1920, and then moving on to the sexual revolution in the '60s and '70s with the introduction of the birth control pill and the women's liberation movement. Now today, the question is, why, in the twenty-first century, are we still chasing equality? It seems we must keep our boots on the ground with any new arguments arising regarding the rights we already have won. Do we need another seismic shift in attitude? Why are we still fighting for a woman's worth?

I hope this book can be an eye-opener for many women around the world, because the more conscious we become of the difference that we can make by standing up for our rights, then the more rights we can pass onto our daughters, granddaughters, and all who succeed us.

Women have achieved a great deal in the last one hundred years, for which I am very thankful. I'd like a guarantee that those types of struggles will never be necessary again. So let us take a look at all the wonderful accomplishments women—the groundbreakers, the trailblazers, women who have shaped the world we now live in—have made over those years. Let us honor them and thank them for their courage and bravery that has led the way to the life we can live today. It is because I am a woman I suggest just how empowering we as women can be, whether as an individual or as a gathering of many.

Remember the brave women of the past who fought for us; they battled so that all women of all color could have the vote—imagine not having that! In some countries they still don't! And also, keep in mind the courageous women of today who are still trying to move on through the still-standing political and religious barriers all over the world. Let us just all keep moving on and remember the words of Helen Reddy:

I am woman, hear me roar!

CHAPTER 2

New-Age Alert

I feel an uprising is on the horizon: the new-age woman is active, smart, and enjoying the many equal rights handed down from her ancestors. Now technology has brought her into a further evolved existence. She is a savvy, modern woman and is now aware of many more political issues via the social media that have at times been accompanied by scattered attempts within branches of political groups to take away some of her rights already fought for and passed as law. Politicians are beginning to become scrutinized and exposed, and are now more transparent than ever, thanks to the ever-evolving technology.

The realization of this has hit today's woman smack in the face, as there has been a quiet on the shore for many years, since the pioneer fellow women, mothers, and grandmothers picketed, protested, and screamed bloody murder for their and all women's sakes. In the 1960s and '70s, the women's liberation movement was also sometimes seen as synonymous with radical feminism, as both movements were concerned with freeing members of society from an oppressive social structure. This book is about a consciousness of equality reflecting many different areas in life, with *respect* for women being of the highest priority. Without that, our worth dwindles.

I have given considerable thought on how I should create this book, as it contains my personal thoughts, feelings, and facts that I have researched. Yes, women's rights have come a long way, but do we realize just how far and what a struggle the journey has been? I have lived and practiced this book, and the only way I feel I can start is with a realistic overview of all the wonderful and the horrific stories that reveal the facts regarding the fight for equality for women around the world. There has been a mind-set over the centuries regarding a woman's position in society, and the result of that has been that we have had to fight to have the same rights as a man. I might mention that this is also the way of thinking with regard to minority groups and civil rights movements that are forever fighting for the people's civil liberties.

But in this book, I will discuss women's progressive rights. We are not second-best, and, if nothing else, this book will show you just that. Your self-worth and how you see yourself is the key to all your rights: if you do not feel that you are worthy, then you will not be seen as worth the right. I have thought that women need to show passion regarding the fight for their personal rights and the rights of all women; thus, I am revealing the many stages we have collectively passed through over the years that have caused great pain, humiliation, and even death. I will try to show what the empowerment of women has resulted in and the great hurdles they have climbed.

Being a woman is a wonderful thing; we have been compared to Venus, Cleopatra, and other queens and goddesses. Since the beginning of time, poets and songwriters have written beautiful poems about women's beauty and love. Woman gives life, nurtures, prepares a nest, and perhaps loves a partner and their children; therefore, she should be worshiped, adored, and praised to high heaven for all her precious and goddess-like attributes.

On top of all that, in today's age the presence of women in the workplace has increased greatly due to many reasons, such as social, domestic, or economic. Either way, she goes to work and puts in a full day either outside or in the home; shops, feeds, and bathes her lot; does the laundry; helps with homework; and eventually drops herself into bed, so that she can get up in a few hours to begin the same duties again.

To be fair, there is now a new generation of men sprouting up who are more congenial to assisting with the "nesting chores" and other types of responsibilities of marriage and home life, and most of them too are not aware of the history of the fight for women's rights. The changing times have been a hard turnaround for men—a duel so to speak, between what feels "natural" to them and how the world of women has evolved into what was once a "man's world." Everything takes time, and this too shall pass, and perhaps with their support, the life for their goddesses will become easier in due time.

All that being said, what the hell happened to equal pay? Don't even try to take away my birth control and my personal rights of choice, and please protect me from gender violence! If anyone ever deserved a break today, it's *you*, baby. So hang in there.

Something like a seismic shift or aftershock is occurring regarding politically imposed restrictions on women's right to choose and equal-pay issues. Mostly, I believe that the majority of the suggested restrictions have been driven by religious belief, the good-old-boy attitude, and not being able to let go of the old ways; remember, the separation of church and state is the distance in the relationship between organized religion and the nation-state.

Suggestive of a harsh comparison, enter the horrible reminder of England's King Henry VIII reign, and that, if any resemblance of that time should return again, even in the most miniscule way, this was enough to disturb my gastrointestinal tract seriously. He created his own religion to enable him to control state and religious rights that involved, of course, his many wives and "off with your head!" Again, these women had no rights at all. (Imagine that!)

Even with those days long gone, we still seem to be living in a puritanical society in this new age of the twenty-first century (compared to some countries), where some groups are still living in an age gone by stuck in their Stone Age way of thinking and are not keeping up with today's cultural diversity and evolving society that is changing the world as fast as is technology.

We all know that even today, in parts of the Middle East and some third-world countries, women still have drastically fewer civil rights than we do in the Western world. There are many women's civil rights organizations whose collective voice has changed the world in different ways and impacted many women's lives for the better. The women in those countries have been stripped of all dignity and are not aware that they too have rights. The great accomplishment of these active organizations can now mean that those women have been given to realize that they do not have to live in the cruel ways they have submitted to for centuries and that we hope help is on the way. We as women will rally throughout the world to support and protect these third-world women, so that we all may have the just and human rights we were all meant to have, not just a select few. As in the Arab Spring, now we hope for a "Woman's Spring." Join hands across the world, and we will conquer.

I am a woman, and I am proud of it: we have come a long way through all the changes, trials, and triumphs through the ages, but we have further to go and more work ahead of us all; and we need to work together as a community with a common goal, not just for ourselves, but for all future women, to show them how to be strong and to stand firm to fight for what they believe in, and to nurture their self-worth, because, without that, they will not feel worthy.

Women typically go through life just nesting and taking care of their families, not to mention their professional workloads. Somewhere along the line, we tend to forget ourselves and sometimes lose our own personal identity. So who on earth has time to "fight for rights"? For centuries, the majority of us have had to just accept what is before us and get on with it. So, extending a helping hand either alone or collaboratively within an organization, we must recognize the trailblazers and groundbreakers of the world as they continue to show us the way.

When I came to the USA from England in 1966, it was the time of the second woman's revolution, the "sexual revolution," which was driven mostly by college students and the feminist movement; oh yes, talk was about time to "burn the bra" but what did that really mean? That is somewhat of a myth due to the 1968 Miss America pageant and the radical women's movement that only wanted to proclaim, "Let's judge ourselves as people." This was also the time of the Vietnam draft card burnings, and somehow the bra burning became related to that at that time. This was the age of the Pill: woman finally gained sole and exclusive power over her fertility. Would that have appealed to your great-grandmother?

Soon to follow was Roe vs. Wade, the 1973 Supreme Court case that gave women the right to have an abortion in specific situations. Today we still feel we have to cling on to these changes by fighting legislation all the time. These issues may not be a priority to all women, but, as a majority, women do not want to lose the right to choose what they feel is right for them as an individual.

So, we have had a couple of mighty evolutionary storms in the name of women's rights over the past two centuries; then there was a quiet lull—not discounting the woman's rights organizations that have always been active, but I feel, after talking to my peers and women of all age groups, some awareness became lost in women's busy lives, and a large portion of women in all age groups and communities just couldn't keep up or perhaps became complacent with life as it was.

Now in this election year of 2012, I feel the *aftershock* coming on again: a new awareness has awakened in the women of today. The new-age woman is paying attention to the several controversial political statements that were made that have had threatening attitudes. So, if we do not want to lose our existing rights, and if we want to ensure that we keep them, well, ladies, you just have to think about how you would feel if you did not have any of these rights now that were gained for you by blood, sweat, and tears of women gone by. Don't even let us get close to that situation, girlfriend: be the best you can be, stand up for your rights, and ROAR like a bloody lioness protecting her cubs, because that is exactly what you must do to keep and protect your children and all the young women who will follow you.

As I said, I am just a believer of equality for all. My subject happens to be centered on women, to reveal some of what has had to happen over the years to move us forward and to give us a better perspective on what women's rights are, and as a reminder for many of us regarding what had to happen to give us the life we have today.

CHAPTER 3

Women's Suffrage

Suffrage is the civil right to vote and to run for office

What does today's woman understand about suffrage and the importance of the Nineteenth Amendment?

How many movies or books have depicted women as a second-rate social character over the centuries? We really do not have to go far back into history to see how real all those facts and situations were. Up until the early nineteen hundreds, women had very little rights inclusive of their children, property, or just themselves. When married, a woman was considered chattel or property. She was financially supported, and, as the majority of women then did not work, had no profession and was not expected to pursue one; she had no choice but to obey (hence the marriage vows). If she did not, then she was threatened to be thrown out onto the streets, where, in the earlier centuries, she had a choice then to either starve or sell herself for a loaf of bread, and, if she was caught, she was probably thrown in jail. She had no right to vote, there was no birth control, there were many children she could not afford or take care of, and death upon giving birth was commonplace, as was the early death of the infant.

A woman's hardships and grief were many, and so out of that rose the women's suffrage movement by the courageous women noted in history. The fight was on for "the vote" and many other rights that women did not have.

In 1848, the demand for women's vote was formulated and then continued on after the Civil War ended in 1865, but then the proposed Fifteenth Amendment to the constitution gave the vote to black men after emancipation and not to women. The Fifteenth Amendment prohibits the denial of the right to vote based on race, color, or previous condition of servitude. In the US, campaigners or "suffragettes" such as Susan B. Anthony and Elizabeth Cady Stanton refused to endorse the amendment, *as it did not give the vote to women.* Others, such as Lucy Stone and Julia Ward Howe, also refused.

And so, fifty-one years later, after the Thirteenth Amendment for emancipation went into effect, women got to vote!

Women's suffrage in the United States was achieved gradually, at state and local levels, during the late nineteenth century and early twentieth century, culminating in 1920 with the passage of the *Nineteenth Amendment* to the United States Constitution, which provided that

> the right of citizens of the United States to vote shall not be denied or abridged by the United States or by any State on account of sex.

Along with the fight for the vote were many other issues of equality, and some of the laws reviewed were reflected back to Britain where they originated.

The Married Women's Property Act of 1882 was an Act of the Parliament of the United Kingdom that significantly altered English law regarding the property rights granted to married women. This allowed women to own and control their own property. Susan B. Anthony also fought for these rights as a collaborative effort for all women.

Once an English woman became married, her husband and herself became one person under the law, and, as the property of the wife was surrendered to her husband, her legal identity ceased to exist. English law defined the role of the wife as a "covered" woman, or, in other words, taken care of by the master, emphasizing passiveness and that the husband then became her "leader"; she was considered to be lower status.

If she chose to remain single, then she was equal to a man in the eyes of the law. Women who never married or who were widowed maintained control over their property and inheritance, owned land and controlled property disposal; once married, the only way that women could reclaim property was through widowhood. Any personal property acquired by the wife during the marriage, unless specified that it was for her own separate use, went automatically to her husband. Married women were unable to draft wills or dispose of any property without their husbands' consent.

Women were often limited in what they could inherit. Males were more likely to receive real property (land), while females with brothers were sometimes limited to inherited personal property, which included clothing, jewelry, household furniture, food, and all moveable goods.

In an instance where no will was found, the English law automatically gave the oldest son the right to all real property, and the daughter inherited only real (as opposed to personal) property in the absence of a male heir. This law remained on the English law books until 1927.

The dissolution of a marriage, whether initiated by the husband or wife, usually left the divorced females impoverished and sometimes destitute, as the law offered them no rights to marital property. They were looked down upon and lost all respectability. That eventually resulted in the Married Women's Property Act of 1882:

> By marriage, the personal identity
> of the woman is lost. Her person
> is completely sunk in that of her
> husband, and he acquires an
> absolute mastery over her person

and effects. Hence her complete disability to contract legal obligations; and except in the event of separation by divorce, or other causes, a married woman in the United Kingdom cannot engage in trade. (Leone Levi, *International Commercial Law*, 1863)

After that time, when an American heiress married into a British titled family, an exchange of "fortune vs. title" would be the purpose, and this would then enable the "line of peerage" to continue without financial difficulty.

In 1895, nine American heiresses married titled British men, including a duke, an earl, and three barons. But soon there emerged a flaw in the plan: the English legal system allowed only the eldest son a title and put him in line to inherit a greater one. Sir Winston Leonard Spencer Churchill (British prime minister during World War II) was the son of Lord Randolph Churchill and an American mother, Jeanette Jerome from Brooklyn, who became Lady Randolph

Churchill in 1874.

In the nineteenth century, limited voting rights were gained in Sweden, Finland, Britain, and some of the western United States. The first European country to introduce women's suffrage was the Grand Duchy of Finland (the predecessor state of modern Finland. It existed 1809–1917 as part of the Russian Empire and was ruled by the Russian emperor as grand prince). In 1893 the very first nation to extend voting rights to adult women was New Zealand, and South Australia became the first to obtain for women the right to run for parliament.

The American Women's Suffrage Association and the National Women's Suffrage Association at that time also campaigned for married women to be given property rights. Now, I am a woman of substance. Thank you!

Opposition to women's rights in the United States at that time included men and women who believed that women voters would close the saloons—now, *that* would have been sad! Then there were the southern white men who were afraid that black women would get the vote—imagine that!

There were ethnic politicians, especially Catholics, whose women were not allowed a political voice. Another problem for the Equal Rights Association was funding. It took a good deal of money to rent halls for speeches, print pamphlets, and pay suffrage workers.

Most of the contributors, however, were female volunteers without incomes. Susan B. Anthony said, "Neither the radical republicans nor Old Abolitionists, nor yet do the Democrats open their purses, pulpits or presses to our movement."

Who was Susan B. Anthony? We know her name and that she is on a dollar coin (which was meant to replace the dollar bill, but, as the dollar bill is still in circulation, the coin has not yet taken its expected place). Born in Adams, Massachusetts, in 1820 to a Quaker family, her father Daniel was a cotton manufacturer and abolitionist, a stern but open-minded man. It is written that Lucy, Susan's mother, was a strong believer in "the inner spirit" and "self-worth." Perhaps Susan inherited those values that led her to her life's work towards the women's suffrage movement. She later pulled away from her family Quaker religion and became an agnostic. She also campaigned for the abolition of slavery and the right for women to own their own property and retain their earnings. She never married. Susan B. Anthony campaigned for a constitutional amendment affirming that women had the right to vote, but died in the first decade of the twentieth century without ever casting a legal ballot.

Suffragettes not only lobbied but also conducted marches, political boycotts, picketing of the White House, and civil disobedience. As a result, they were attacked, arrested, imprisoned, force-fed, raped in prisons, and beaten. But the country's conscience was stirred, and the support for women's suffrage grew. There were many key events and dedicated suffragettes between 1848 and 1920, but the most famed event was *the Seneca Falls, NY, women's rights convention, the first ever held. It set the agenda for the women's rights movement.* This all took place approximately seventy years before the signing of the Nineteenth Amendment.

In the 1960s, one of the main influential resources was the Commission on the Status of Women founded by Eleanor Roosevelt in 1961. She was appointed by President John F. Kennedy, but, while in the Senate, it had been noted Kennedy had voted against laws to give women more equality. But after a private meeting with the former first lady, she convinced him of the need for equality for women. Go, Eleanor!

The world's history has been a long and messy crawl toward equal suffrage for all. Each and every group outside of the wealthy elite has had to fight to have their voices heard. Clearly, there is an obvious change in the various demographics that are coming out to vote. Women of all groups are taking up political office, and their voices are being heard. Where the clear major voice in America once was the white male, now that one voice is giving way to Hispanics and women, primarily. It's not completely there yet, but it just seems a matter of time until the playing field is completely neutral. After all this changing from what we once called the "minority voice," women are now representing the largest sector of what once was not an influence, but now is. Political parties will need to understand this in order to move forward.

It's great that women are voting in large numbers; that alone would make the suffragettes very proud of how women voters have changed the way that America and the world votes, now and going into the future.

"I am Woman"

Song by

Helen Reddy
I am woman, hear me roar
in numbers too big to ignore,
and I know too much to go back and
pretend.

'Cause I've heard it all before
and I've been down on the floor;
no one's ever gonna keep me down again.

Oh yes, I am wise,
but it's wisdom born of pain.
Yes I've paid the price,
but look how much I've gained.

If I have to, I can do anything:
I am strong.
I am invincible.
I am woman.

Dedicated to all the suffragettes

CHAPTER 4

Changes

The only constant in life is change.

We have come a long way since the days when women discovered they could fight for their rights. Now, we'll move forward and review some of the changes into the twenty-first century.

Up until the middle to late '60s, family life in some parts of the Western world resembled *Leave It to Beaver*, a TV series set in the late '50s. Typically, the mother, June, was at home, cooking and cleaning house, and usually in high heels and a nice dress and covered by an apron—oh, and presenting her husband with a cocktail upon his arrival from a hard day's work.

I fully respect that scenario, as it used to be mine to a degree, but, at that time, it was still what was expected, as most women still did not work. The mind-set was still that the man would take care of the woman financially, and she would stay home and raise the family. That was just the way it was done then. The problem with that was that the majority of the women did not learn a trade or skill while married, and, if there was trouble in their marriages, they had no way to survive after divorce.

There were some options arising at that time beyond being a shop girl, such as nursing or going to secretarial school. Those professions were encouraged at that time as a suitable job for a woman. (*Mad Men*, the TV series, will show you that many women at that time needed to be on the subservient side to keep a job.) Sexual harassment was common, but not much was done about that then, as it was considered a male-dominated world and no one wanted to lose the option of being able to put food on the table.

This then only added to the feeling of being trapped for some women who were being treated badly by drunken, abusive husbands who strayed. Some men just walked out and left their wives with children, no incomes, and stranded, without jobs to go to. Divorce became prominent, and, while women struggled to survive with their children, many husbands left without giving any support. Even though in 1910 a federal law was approved, by twenty-four jurisdictions, making it a crime for husbands to abandon or neglect their children, the law didn't provide recourse for parents who left the jurisdiction; these parents frequently escaped justice by relocating to a jurisdiction that hadn't adopted the law.

This book is not about men and their behavior; the truth speaks for itself. It is about women and how they didn't want to take it anymore! As the revolution evolved into the '70s and '80s, work became more available for women. However, the pay was less than it should have been, and the hours were long, and many women had to leave the children home with sitters or sometimes alone (then called "latch key kids"), so their mothers could make a living.

So now we take a look at what exactly has changed? We know that *Planned Parenthood and the Pill* and other methods of birth control have been revolutionary. Enovid, the first birth-control pill, went on the market in 1960. Unlike any other previously available form of contraception, the Pill was both reliable and controlled by a woman herself, requiring neither the consent nor the knowledge of her sexual partner. Within five years, six million American and British women were on the Pill. With one quick visit to a doctor, a woman immediately gained sole and exclusive power over her fertility, a power that had eluded her sex since the beginning of time. Women were now liberated, and the Pill steeply lowered the risks of accidental fatherhood and unwanted marriage.

Not to ignore that, before the 1960s and the newly released Pill, sex before marriage came with high risk and much discrimination. An unmarried woman risked pregnancy, and with pregnancy came a limited number of unsavory, life-changing options: an illegal abortion of doubtful safety, a shotgun wedding, forced adoption, or single motherhood of a child whose birth certificate would be stamped for posterity with the word *illegitimate*.

A US federal law *prohibiting sexual harassment in the workplace* was amended in the 1964 Civil Rights Act. The amendment to the law makes certain employers responsible for preventing and stopping sexual harassment that occurs on the job. The amendment applies to private and most public employers, labor organizations, employment agencies, and joint employer-union apprenticeship programs with fifteen or more employees.

Not only is sexual harassment now against the law, but also, so is retaliating (taking revenge) against someone for complaining about sexual harassment or for participating in an investigation of sexual harassment. (Good-bye to the 1950s!)

Examples of retaliation include the following: If a woman complained about sexual harassment, she was made to take an unpaid leave of absence, and the harasser continued to work; or, after she wrote a letter describing the sexual harassment that she witnessed and was subject to, she was reassigned to a less desirable position in the same or a different department.

Then there was *Roe v. Wade.* Roe v. Wade was the 1973 Supreme Court case that gave women the right to have an abortion. Before this case, it was illegal for women to have abortions without extenuating circumstances. This extremely controversial case legalized abortion in the first trimester of pregnancy, or before the fetus becomes viable. Pro-life groups debate that life begins at conception (as does the Catholic Church), whereas other groups defend their position of different stages of viability. Today, in 2013, Roe v. Wade law is forty years old, and religious and political groups continue to threaten to overturn this law through Supreme Court rule.

The history of the case of "Jane Roe" Norma L. McCorvey was established in Texas, in 1970, where she claimed her pregnancy was the result of a rape. The defendant in the case was Dallas County District Attorney Henry Wade, representing the state of Texas. The US Supreme court issued its decision on January 22, 1973, with a seven to two majority voting to strike down Texas abortion laws.

Abortion before Roe had been subject to *criminal statutes* since at least the nineteenth century, as women at that time had no choice but to either subject themselves to "back alley" procedures or a self-inflicted coat hanger, which many times resulted in death. What say I; what say you? *Plenty!* Today forty-one states prohibit abortions generally, except when necessary to protect the woman's life or health, after a specified point in pregnancy, most often fetal viability. Thirty-nine states require an abortion to be performed by a licensed physician. Twenty-one states require an abortion to be performed in a hospital after a specified point in the pregnancy, and nineteen states require the involvement of a second physician after a specified point.

So are the changes good or bad; this is in the eye of the beholder.

Then there is the *equal pay for women* issue regarding pay inequality between men and women. There has been much data over the years, mostly dealing with English-speaking territories; this was not a worldwide study but did show the median wage for women is lower than the median wage for men in the studied countries.

A **gender pay gap** study by country revealed the countries of women who were the highest paid and had the lowest gender pay gap is as follows in alphabetical order.

1. Australia: "equal pay for work of equal value" by women was introduced in 1969. Anti-discrimination on the basis of sex was legislated in 1984.

2. Canada: the Canadian Human Rights Act is a statute passed by the Parliament of Canada in 1977.

3. Ireland: the Anti-Discrimination (Pay) Act was passed in 1974 and came into force in 1977.

4. United Kingdom: the Equal Pay Act of 1970 was passed by the United Kingdom parliament.

5. United States: *In 1963*, Congress passed the Equal Pay Act as an amendment to the Fair Labor Standards Act, to prohibit discrimination on account of sex in the payment of wages by employers.

The Lilly Ledbetter Fair Pay Act. This US bill was finally signed into law in 2009 by President Barack Obama. What does this mean? The act would allow pay discrimination lawsuits to proceed years or even decades after alleged discrimination took place. The bill's purpose is to close a loophole in an American law intended to protect women and racial minorities from pay discrimination. It amends the Civil Rights Act of 1964 to include lawsuits initiated within 180 days of discrimination, as opposed to the old rule, which set the statute's limitations at 180 days from the initial discrimination.

Before the Lily Ledbetter Fair Pay Act, if an employer could conceal the discrimination for that time period, the employee would have no recourse. Now lawsuits can be filed within 180 days of the last incident of discrimination.

What about the changes for *the women in the military*? The number of women in the military has increased by 20 percent, and, although there is still some resistance in the Pentagon, the ban on women to be allowed to go to "the front" is about to be lifted. Women have done so before, such as in Israel, and successfully so. It is also being discussed that, as the assault incidence on female recruits is still of great concern, the reports will be channeled via an independent entity rather than the chain of command. This will greatly assist in nondiscriminatory justice.

Those days seem to have passed us by like ships on the sea; the labels are gone, and single motherhood is much accepted now, just as interracial marriage and gay rights have progressed to the modern era.

As of 2011, girls born to a British heir to the throne will be equal in throne succession: After three hundred years under old succession laws, sons and daughters of any future British monarch will have equal right to the throne, after Commonwealth leaders have agreed to change succession laws. The idea that a younger son should become monarch instead of an elder daughter because he is a man—this way of thinking is in line for collision with the modern world that we have become.

The men and woman of today are far more accepting of all these evolving changes, and they do not see them to be so strange or outrageous anymore, as it had been for the earlier generations. The woman today is an advocate of free choice to have the same rights as a man; it isn't really so important what the issue is, but it is a matter of being given the choice, so that she *may* choose.

We are going through a changing society—an evolution of society, you might say, and with this comes a new-age way of thinking and acceptance of equality. Today, if a woman wishes to stay home and raise her children—and many women do—she has so much more protection and many rights passed down to her to make her life much easier if problems do occur.

Therefore, that gives the woman of today the right to choose whether she wants to work or not, without the fear the woman of yesterday had to face.

As an added note, if Thomas Jefferson's

phrase in the Declaration of Independence stating **"all men are created equal"** would have included women, then perhaps equality would not have been so much of a problem!

Bob Dylan's celebrated song titled "The Times, They Are a-Changin'" in 1964 reflected issues of concern such as racism, poverty, and social change for all groups.

2012: And they still are a-changing!

CHAPTER 5

Violence against Women

Since the "Violence against Women Act" (VAWA) was passed into law by President Bill Clinton on September 13, 1994, VAWA has provided life-saving assistance to millions of women and families across the nation. For battered women, the law has provided critical law-enforcement protections and often a way out from a life of abuse.

VAWA provided $1.6 billion toward investigation and prosecution of violent crimes against women. Specifically, the bill included increased protections for women on college campuses across the nation, following the brutal 2010 murder of a young woman at the University of Virginia.

VAWA's 2012 renewal was opposed by conservative Republicans, who objected to extending the act's protections to same-sex couples and to provisions allowing battered illegal immigrants to claim temporary visas.

Provisions of the Senate bill would protect gay men, lesbians, American Indians living in reservations, and illegal immigrants who were victims of domestic violence. The new law-enforcement measures were to safeguard women on tribal reservations, one in three of whom will be raped in their lifetimes. Also added was nondiscrimination language for those in the LGBT (lesbian, gay, bisexual, and transgender) community, who had been unfairly left out of previous bills. It provided protections to immigrant women, regardless of their status, who are often scared into silence at the hands of their abusers.

Since then, the issue has gone nowhere. The leadership in the House of Representatives allowed the clock to run out on the protections that bill would have provided to millions of women across our country. This House leaders' failure will have real-life implications for women who now find themselves with nowhere to turn for help.

On January 2, 2013, the Senate's 2012 reauthorization of VAWA was not brought up for a vote in the House, effectively ending the bill after eighteen years. VAWA continues to petition to get this passed. This landmark legislation has funded clinics, shelters, and hotlines for victims in crisis across the country, and has provided tools for law enforcement to crack down on abusers and rapists since VAWA was first passed in 1994.

After some review of VAWA and current updates, I can include a list of statistics showing the success of the funding clinics, shelters, and hotlines for victims in crisis across the country.

- Reporting of domestic violence has increased as much as 51 percent.
- All states have passed laws making stalking a crime and have strengthened rape laws.
- The number of individuals killed by an intimate partner has decreased by 34 percent for women and 57 percent for men.
- After using VAWA funding to institute a lethality assessment program, Maryland's intimate partner homicides have been reduced by a remarkable 41 percent over four years.
- A 2010 study demonstrated that an increase in the number of legal services available is associated with a decrease in intimate partner homicide.

- A 2009 Department of Justice study found Kentucky saved $85 million in one alone year through the issuance of protection orders and the reduction in violence they caused.
- VAWA saved $12.6 billion in its first six years alone.
- States have passed more than 660 laws to combat domestic violence, dating violence, sexual assault, and stalking. All states have passed laws making stalking a crime and changed laws that treated date or spousal rape as a lesser crime than stranger rape.
- Since 1996, the National Domestic Violence Hotline has answered over two million calls. The hotline receives over twenty-one thousand calls a month.
- And provides access to translators in 170 languages.
- Businesses also have joined the national fight against violence. Hundreds of companies, led by the model programs established by Altria, Polaroid, Liz Claiborne, The Body Shop, Aetna, and DuPont, have created employee assistance programs that help victims of domestic violence.

- More victims are reporting violence by an intimate partner.

Statistics have shown that women worldwide of all ages are more likely to die or be maimed because of male violence than because of cancer, heart disease, and accidents combined. Weekly international news is riveting with a new rape, or other violent assaults on a woman. Amongst human rights abuses is sex trafficking and prostitution of women and children all over the world. Recently uncovered in the southern United States, news revealed that many female immigrants were lured to the United States and were then threatened with deportation unless they became prostitutes.

We all know the world is not a perfect place, and that there have been many assaults on different groups of people for decades; namely, LGBT rights, racism for different ethnic groups, women's rights, and don't forget how interracial marriage was banned at one time (that, again, is another story). All these have been defended by the human and civil rights activists. It's an ongoing battle for equal rights for all groups. Although moving along slowly, we are getting there; we just cannot give up. The frustrating part of it all is that just when you feel something has been accomplished for the good, another rude awakening raises its ugly head.

Will the human race ever get it right! We must keep moving forward, conquering and preventing the atrocities on women and girls around the world from happening. Fight for what *you* believe in!

Horrific news of a woman's gang rape attack in India traveled the world; we do not need to further discuss the details, we all know how we feel about that. It's 2013, and the brutal, global war on women must stop. We can start by drawing the line in India and other countries not recognizing that this kind of brutality is *not* acceptable anywhere.

The fifteen-year-old girl from Pakistan shot in the head by the Taliban has become an internationally recognized symbol of resistance to the Taliban's efforts to deny women education and other rights. More than 250,000 people have signed online petitions calling for her to be nominated for a Nobel Peace Prize for her activism.

Recently the news announced the case of the sixteen-year-old high school teenager in Ohio who was at a party and allegedly raped by boys in the football team. The case is still under investigation, and the town of Steubenville says that it is not the first time a high school football team has been entangled in accusations of sexual assault. It is a sexual assault accusation in the age of social media, when teenagers are capturing much of their lives on their camera phones. No doubt, the outcome will be long and arduous.

All this is about power and control by the attackers, and this type of assault happens everywhere in the world. We cannot control it all, but we can continue to try to put legislation into place to provide more tools to fight it, give better council to overcome it, and to support the victims and show them there is no shame in their assault. If all women stood as *one* body, then we could make a universal difference.

On March 3, 1989, a man wearing a ski mask entered Debbie Smith's Williamsburg, Virginia, home and threatened her with a gun, dragged her into the woods, blindfolded her, and raped her repeatedly over the next hour. She participated in the collection of DNA evidence for a rape kit, but it was not until five years after the victim's assault, on

July 24, 1995, that a DNA technician identified Debbie's attacker.

This resulted in the Debbie Smith DNA Backlog Program. The Debbie Smith Act of 2004 provides United States federal government grants to eligible states and units of local government to conduct DNA analyses of backlogged DNA samples collected from victims of crimes and criminal offenders. The act expands the Combined DNA Index Systems and provides legal assistance to survivors of dating violence.

An October 2008 audit of the Los Angeles city crime lab by Human Rights Watch revealed that rape kit backlogs increased between 2004 and 2008, despite nearly $4 million in funds from the Debbie Smith DNA Backlog Program. (This data may have changed since researched.)

According to a 2009 news investigation, at least twenty thousand untested rape kits were being held in four major US cities, and an additional twelve major cities had no idea how many rape kits remained untested in law-enforcement storage facilities.

So what are we to conclude with all this information? The numbers clearly show that at least twenty thousand rapes occurred in a few states during the years 2004–2009 and still there is a backlog on rape kits with $4 million in funding.

Do the numbers show that violence against women has decreased? Or do we women still have a big fight on our hands for protection and justice following "the crime without shame"? It is here, it is there, it is everywhere. Is this politically driven on a funding level? How important is the crime of rape really thought to be? I see no evidence of us women being the highest priority. What is the problem?

Definition of Rape: the unlawful compelling of a person through physical force or duress to have sexual intercourse.

Assault, in law, is an attempt or threat, going beyond mere words, to use violence, with the intent and apparent ability to do harm to another. If violent contact actually occurs, the offense of battery has been committed; modern criminal statutes often combine assault and battery. Modern criminal statutes recognize certain degrees of assault (e.g., with intent to kill, to do great bodily harm, to rape) as aggravated assaults and felonies.

Review of many still-standing old laws in the US show that discrimination toward women is still in effect. *Laws as far back as 1872 have been revealed;* one recent court case came to the attention of the media regarding a rape that occurred in California of a single woman: the law apparently states that because she is an unmarried woman, *it is not considered rape*! The case is shedding light on a legal loophole that protects some rapists who prey on unmarried women. Lawmakers who have allowed the loophole to remain on the books are under fire.

This is 2013. Get those laws off the books, do your job, and let us *please* move on!

To conclude, *yes*, we have come a long way, and there are many coalitions for women's rights all over the world today, and in the future I am sure we will still be moving forward toward our goals; but we will continue to have a struggle before we get to the point of women feeling safe from assault and brutality and justly protected.

CHAPTER 6

Female Trailblazers

In the evolution of women's rights over the past few decades, we know of great women who have been called groundbreakers or trailblazers for their amazing accomplishments in their lifetimes, paving the way for others to follow—women who have climbed high in all professions, especially the military, politics, civil rights, and business. The election of women leaders around the world has grown and has been widely accepted.

Positions for women holding office in politics have increased. Women are becoming more and more powerful in deciding the direction of this country and the world over. Women in the US made up 54 percent of the electorate in the 2012 election, and the results were very encouraging. There will now be seventy-eight women in the House of Representatives, and, for the first time in US history, twenty female senators. The 2012 elections saw eleven women elected to the Senate. Nancy Pelosi remains in the position of Democratic minority leader. There have been three female secretaries of state, the current one being Hillary Clinton, and many women in the US are visualizing that she may become the first women presidential candidate in the coming years. Currently, three women hold position as Supreme Court Justices. These numbers clearly show how women have persevered and surged forward.

The number of female CEOs has increased greatly in the US. There are now twenty female CEOs running America's largest companies, and more than half landed the top job between 2011 and 2012.

Marissa Ann Mayer is an American business executive. As of 2012, she is the president and CEO of Yahoo! Previously, she was a long-time executive and key spokesperson for Google. She is the youngest CEO of a Fortune 500 company, and has been ranked number fourteen on the list of America's most powerful businesswomen of 2012 by *Fortune* magazine. IBM changed its hundred- year male-only track record and in 2012 appointed a woman, Ginni Rometty, to lead the company. Wal-Mart appointed Rosalind Brewer as its first woman and first

African-American to head a subsidiary company, Sam's Club.

Women in the media have excelled in many ways—journalism, civil rights, and philanthropy—such as; Oprah Winfrey's rising from poverty to become the first African-American woman billionaire; Oprah Winfrey embodies the American dream. Through television, movies, books, and radio, she speaks to women the world over.

Christiane Amanpour is currently working as CNN's chief international consultant, most widely known for her up-close coverage of the Middle East, beginning with the Gulf War in 1990. She is globally recognized as one of the most influential international correspondents in the world, due partly to her willingness to report from dangerous situations.

Civil rights activists such as Aung San Suu Kyi have fought courageously for human rights and democracy; she is the world's only Nobel Peace Prize recipient currently imprisoned. She is the leader of the National League for Democracy in Burma, and has been imprisoned by the country's military dictatorship off-and-on since July of 1989.

Advocating nonviolent resistance in the tradition of Mohandas Gandhi and Dr. Martin Luther King Jr., Suu Kyi has refused to accept freedom in exchange for banishment from her country. She was awarded the Nobel Peace Prize in 1991.

My special addition as trailblazer is fifteen-year-old Malala Yousufzai from Pakistan, who recently was shot in the head by the Taliban for daring to say girls should be able to get an education. This shocking story shows just how far we in the Western world have come, and just how far other countries have to go.

Some other "firsts" for women in the past three decades have been recognized as major leaps toward equality for women in professions traditionally dominated by men. Taking a glimpse from back to the 1980s, we can see many immense accomplishments:

1981   Sandra Day O'Connor was appointed by President Reagan to the Supreme Court, making her its first woman justice.

1983   On June 18, Sally Ride became the first American woman astronaut to travel in space for a six-day mission aboard the space shuttle *Challenger*.

1985   Penny Harrington becomes the first female police chief of a major US city (Portland, Oregon).

1986   Ann Bancroft of Minnesota becomes the first woman to walk to the North Pole.

1987   The National Museum for Women in the Arts opens in Washington, DC.

The "Queen of Soul" singer Aretha Franklin becomes the first woman inducted into the Rock and Roll Hall of Fame. Her song "Respect" was a huge success.

Then there was the first celebration of Women's History Month in March, a month-long national celebration in the United States.

1989   Ileana Ros-Lehtinen of Florida becomes the first Hispanic woman elected to Congress. She serves in the US House of Representatives.

Dr. Antonia Novello is sworn in as US Surgeon General, becoming the first woman (and first Hispanic) to hold that job.

1992   Carol Moseley-Braun of Illinois becomes the first African-American woman elected to the US Senate.

1993   Toni Morrison becomes the first African-American woman to win the Nobel Prize for literature.

Janet Reno is confirmed by the Senate as US Attorney General, becoming the first woman to hold that job.

1995   Nancy Ruth Mace is the first female cadet to graduate from the Citadel, the formerly all-male military school in South Carolina.

Madeleine Korbelová Albright was the first woman to become the United States Secretary of State. She was nominated by US President Bill Clinton on December 5, 1996, and was unanimously confirmed by a U.S. Senate vote of 99–0. She was sworn in on January 23, 1997.

1999   Lt. Colonel Eileen Collins is the first woman astronaut to command a space-shuttle mission. Collins had also been the first woman to pilot a space shuttle.

2002   Halle Berry becomes the first African American to win a Best Actress Academy Award, for her role in *Monster's Ball.*

2012   Air Force Lt. Gen. Janet Wolfenbarger's promotion made her the first female four-star general in Air Force history.

Of course there are many more women to honor as pioneers from the past and the present in all categories and from all over the world, but the above list names just a few to bring to attention to how we women are moving our course through life to gain and keep respect, dignity, and equality for all time.

In my eyes, all women are trailblazers in their own way; let us not discount what they need to accomplish in their lifetime to keep a family together and to give love, guidance, and the sacrifices they make for their loved ones. She blazes the trail for her family to follow. That is what we must honor.

CHAPTER 7

Female Political Leaders

Indira Gandhi: prime minister of India.
Indira Gandhi was the daughter of
Jawaharlal Nehru, India's first prime
minister. She joined her father's Congress
Party in 1938 and was jailed for a while by
the British for her support of India's
independence from Great Britain. After her
father's death, she was elected to parliament
in his place, becoming prime minister
herself in 1966. India endured great
economic troubles during her watch, and,
over time, she lost elections and was
reelected, but in 1984 she met a brutal death
at the hands of Sikh assassins.

Golda Meir: prime minister of Israel. Golda
Meir was born in the Ukraine and lived for a
while in the United States. She immigrated
to Israel in 1921.When Israel became a state,
she was elected to the Knesset (parliament);
in 1969, she was elected prime minister, a
political feat for an Israeli woman at that
time. She was a powerful, tough leader.

*Margaret Thatcher: prime minister of
England.* Margaret Thatcher was Britain's

first female prime minister; elected in 1979, she was the first British prime minister in the twentieth century to win three consecutive terms. She earned the nickname the Iron Lady because of her hard line against the USSR over their invasion of Afghanistan, and because, when Argentina challenged Britain's right to the Falkland Islands, she went to war. In 1990 she resigned as prime minister.

Cristina Elisabet Fernández de Kirchner: president of Argentina. She is Argentina's first elected female president, the second woman to hold the position (after Isabel Martinez de Perón, 1974–1976). Before being elected president of Argentina, Fernandez was a senator, and then the nation's first lady; her husband, Nestor, was elected president in 2003.

Angela Dorothea Merkel: chancellor of Germany. Elected in 2005, Merkel is the first woman chancellor of Germany. In 2007 Merkel was president of the European Council and chaired the G8, the second woman (after Margaret Thatcher) to do so. Angela Merkel has been described as a leader, setting the standards of the European Union, and is currently ranked as the world's second most-powerful person by

Forbes magazine, the highest ranking ever achieved by a woman.

Julia Gillard: prime minister of Australia. Julia Eileen Gillard is an Australian politician who is the twenty-seventh prime minister of Australia and the leader of the Australian Labor Party since 24 June 2010. She is the first woman to hold either office. Gillard was born in Barry, Wales, and migrated with her family to Adelaide, South Australia, in 1966.

Helle Thorning-Schmidt: prime minister of Denmark. Denmark elected its first female prime minister in 2011 and the leader of the Social Democrats since 12 April 2005. She is the first woman to hold either post.

Tarja Kaarina Halonen: prime minister of Finland. Tarja Kaarina Halonen is a Finnish lawyer who was the eleventh president of Finland, serving from 2000 to 2012, and the first female to hold the office. Halonen served as the chairman of Seta, the main LGBT rights organization in Finland. During her presidency, she has participated actively in discussions of women's rights and problems of globalization.

Mary Patricia McAleese: prime minister of

Ireland. She served as the eighth president of Ireland from 1997 to 2011. She was the second female president and was first elected in 1997, succeeding *Mary Robinson*, making McAleese the world's first woman to succeed another as president. She was reelected unopposed for a second term in office in 2004.

President Joyce Banda: President of the Republic of Malawi. President Joyce Banda was successfully sworn in as on 7 April, 2012. The first Malawi female president, Banda has a strong passion for women, children, and the underprivileged. In this regard, she has been involved in development and humanitarian work.

There has been so much advancement for women worldwide since the days of suffrage for women began in the 1800s. I am hoping that I have captured enough of the history— *our* story—although only a small percentage of it, to enable many to see the light, as in the Florence Nightingale lamp, and to show how far we have come through adversity since those days and to be able to reflect fully, and with respect, on how our grandmothers, great-grandmothers, and those before them were forced to live.

Sometimes, when we have something all the time we tend to take it for granted; equality is no different. This is *freedom*, and that should never be taken for granted, because we will become too comfortable, and if we do not keep our eye on the ball, then we may lose the game!

CHAPTER 8

Courage and Love

Caroline Elizabeth Sarah Norton (22 March 1808–15 June 1877): a British feminist, social reformer, and author of the early and mid-nineteenth century.[1]

This is the story of Caroline Norton, a true story of a young woman born in London England in the 1800s. I chose this story because of the documented hardships she endured during her lifetime, when there were no women's rights, and yet she fought for women's rights throughout it all, so that others may not have to live as she had to.

Caroline was born in 1808 into a grand but impoverished family. She was the granddaughter of the playwright Richard Brinsley-Sheridan. Her father died when she was eight years old, leaving the family with serious financial problems. So when George Norton, who was a member of parliament for Guildford at the time, asked to marry Caroline only eight years later, when she was only sixteen, Caroline's mother was anxious for the match to succeed. Against her wishes, but fearing for the well-being of her family, Caroline conceded. The marriage was an extremely miserable one, and Caroline was the victim of regular and vicious beatings and rape. She could not report the abuse, as in those days she would have been informed to adjust to it, as it was a women's duty, and he was the man of the house, the master, and also provided the much-needed finances for the family. This was to be accepted.

She found solace in her writing and the publication of her verses—"The Sorrows of Rosalie" (1829) and "The Undying One" (1830)—resulted in her appointment as editor of *La Belle Assemblée* and *Court Magazine*. With these appointments and publications came a taste of financial independence.

In 1836 she finally left her husband who, in turn, now claimed that Caroline was guilty of adultery with the home secretary, Lord Melbourne, and George Norton sued Melbourne for seducing his wife. Norton lost the case, but Caroline's reputation was ruined. There was no divorce, and Norton refused Caroline access to her three children, and her subsequent protests were instrumental in the passing of *the Infant Custody Bill of 1839.*

Her husband later attempted to take the proceeds of her writing. Her campaign to ensure women were supported after divorce included an eloquent letter to *Queen Victoria, which was published.*

Her writing in verse includes an attack against child labor entitled "Voice from the Factories" (1836), and she also published an autobiographical novel, *Stuart Dunleath* (1851). She dedicated this book to Her Majesty Queen of the Netherlands and wrote,

> The power of writing has always been to me a source of intense pleasure; it has been my best solace in hours of gloom; and the name I have earned as an author in my native land, is the only happy boast of my life.

She was finally able to marry William Stirling Maxwell, her friend for twenty-five years, and sadly, a few months later, she died; it was June 1877.

It is a sad tale of a brave, accomplished woman who was basically forced to marry for money and was brutalized and humiliated. Caroline was unable to obtain a

divorce and was denied access to her three sons. being forced to stalk them.
 Her work would be to write, and eventually that was successful, but, because she was still legally married, her husband could still take her proceeds. At that time, she was seen by many as a famous victim of injustice.

Caroline's efforts were influential in the passing of the Marriage and Divorce Act of 1857. So even though her life began with heartache, it ended with love in her life and the knowledge that other women did not have to suffer as she had.

Now, 135 years later, what would have happened to Caroline today? Can we see just how different her outcome would be?

We can see all she went through and all the rights she did not have then, but she continued to fight for all of us, so that the story of Caroline today would be very different indeed.

We are fortunate to have the freedom that we have, and mostly we no longer have the need to think about it, but what about the less fortunate women of the world—women who do not know this freedom, and women who are still treated badly here in the US and countries all over the world. It is not to say that we all need to become activists or become greatly involved in some group or movement—that is not for everyone—but what we can do is to *pay it forward* to the women next to you on the bus, in the store, the bank; the girl at work, on the elevator, or in the doctor's office. Just say something nice to her, pay her a compliment, and just watch her face light up. You will have given her a *gift* that will make her feel better about herself, and what did I say early on in this book:

Your self-worth and how you see yourself is the key to all your rights; if you do not feel that you are worthy, then you will not be seen as worth the right.

We may not be able to change the world for others all at once, but we can make a difference individually, more than you know.

Two of my favorite movies have come to mind while writing this book; both taught me something that has made me wiser and more aware of who I *am*.

One is the year 2000 movie starring Helen Hunt and Kevin Spacey, *Pay It Forward*, which had an impact on me to where I saw how amazing the effect was just to do one small thing for another and expecting nothing in return. Even a simple smile will work and come right back to you. Just be kind; you do not know what life is like for another woman behind closed doors; sometimes we go around pretending! And there are many tears hiding.

The other is *The Color Purple.* Anyone who has seen this movie will understand the struggle for empowerment that women of all colors and religions, whatever their beliefs are, from all over the world have suffered to gain. The main character in this movie is Celie, who was my hero and inspired me so much. She is a poor, uneducated, fourteen-year-old black girl living in the South. She starts writing letters to God, because her father, Alphonso, beats and rapes her. Alphonso has already impregnated Celie once. Celie gave birth to a girl, whom her father presumably killed in the woods. Celie has a second child, a boy, whom her father also abducts. Celie's mother becomes ill and dies. Alphonso brings home a new wife and continues to abuse Celie.

This story is at the heart of oppression for women over the centuries, and the ending was wonderful and made me cry all over again, this time with joy.

Of course where would we be without the words from my favorite song by Whitney Houston, "The Greatest Love of All"

I decided long ago, never to walk in
anyone's shadow.
If I fail, if I succeed,
At least I live as I believe.
No matter what they take from me,
They can't take away my dignity,
Because the greatest love of all
Is happening to me.
I found the greatest love of all
Inside of me.
The greatest love of all
Is easy to achieve.
Learning to love yourself;
It is the greatest love of all.

In closing, I must say how writing this book has opened my eyes immensely. My mantra is to believe that "I can do it" and keep faith in myself, and that was sometimes a bit of a battle.

I am not a person who practices any religious doctrine, but I do believe that if there is a "higher power," it is pure love and intellect and energy.

I feel and believe that this is within us all,
and if you believe in yourself, you will
believe you are your OWN peace on earth
and that your dignity and your self-esteem is
everything.

You are a woman, and you can be proud of
who you are, share your kindness with
others and grow, grow, grow into old age
knowing you will be passing on your
experiences and knowledge to all those who
have touched your life. Through all that,

the world will be a better place!

Acknowledgments

To my dearest friends who always believed
in me, and to my beloved daughters, who,
without realizing it, helped me to write this
book.

I give great thanks to you all for your faith
in me, for giving me positive encouragement
to keep on going, and standing by me all the
way.

Thank you from my heart with love.

Resources

This book has been based on a large body of research, mostly World Wide Web resources and national and international organizations. Personal opinions and experiences.

Wikipedia Ask.com, answers.yahoo.com, History.com, BBC. History, PBS. World history. Newspaper archives, Google web search.

Organizations contacted: Violence against Women Act (VAWA), National Organization for Women (NOW), Association for Women's Rights in Development (AWID), MADRE, Amnesty International UK/ US, and LGBT Rights.

Sharia, Fatwas, and Women's Rights Global & International Studies .
http://www.global.ucsb.edu/orfaleacenter/lu
ce/luce11/materials/SHARIA.pdf

Famous Women's Rights Activists—
Biography.com
http://www.biography.com/people/groups/ac
tivists/womens-rights-activists.

www.womenforwomen.org

"One woman can change anything. Many women can change everything."

Research and resources provided are updated regularly, and the information provided can be subject to change. Please explore references provided for updated information on "women's rights."

References

Women's **Rights** | LibertyMutual.com
Join a Discussion about one woman's efforts
to empower the oppressed.
http://www.libertymutual.com/Responsibilit
y/

Defend Women's Rights | ncjw.org
Sign up for the NCJW Action Center to
speak out for women and families.
http://www.ncjw.org/Take_Action/

Women Rights Organizations | iZito.com
Search all engines at once for **Women
Rights Organizations** Info
http://izito.com/**Women+Rights+Organizat
ions**/

**National Organization for Women
(NOW)** http://now.org/

MADRE: Demanding rights, resources, and
results for women. MADRE is an
international women's human rights
organization that uses human rights to
advance social justice.
http://www.madre.org/

Association for Women's Rights in Development (AWID)
An international membership organization committed to gender equality and just sustainable development. In English, French, and Spanish.
http://www.awid.org/

Women's Rights Groups in America:|
eHow.com
Connect Women Globally: Org. African Women's Health Center (AWHC) Women's Welfare Associations.

Violence Against Women Act
Ask.comhttp://ask.com/wiki/**Violence Against Women Act** (**VAWA**) « National Domestic Violence ...
http://www.thehotline.org/get-educated/violence-against-women-act-vawa

LGBT Rights
http://www.hrw.org/topic/lgbt-rightshttp:/

Amnesty International UK/US.
"Working to Protect Human Rights"
www.amnesty.org

Caroline Norton's books can be located under the heading **"A Celebration of**

Women Writers," among many other well-known women writers.

www.ingramcontent.com/pod-product-compliance
Lightning Source LLC
Chambersburg PA
CBHW070603290526
45790CB00002B/765